Continue On

Hope and Encouragement
for Every Trusting Heart

By Roy Lessin

Victor

Cook Communications

Victor is an imprint of
Cook Communications Ministries, Colorado Springs, Colorado 80918
Cook Communications, Paris, Ontario
Kingsway Communications, Eastbourne, England

Printed in Singapore.

2 3 4 5 6 7 8 9 10 Printing/Year 04 03 02 01 00

Editor: Roberta Rand
Interior Design: Rini Twait
Cover Design: Brenda Franklin

Library of Congess Cataloging-in-Publication Data

Lessin, Roy.
   Continue on / by Roy Lessin.
      p. cm.
    ISBN 0-7814-3346-0
    1. Christian life--Meditations. I. Title.

 BV4501.2 .L455 2000
 242--dc21

                                                            00-032073

Contents

Introduction

The call of God to our hearts is one of hope and encouragement. He encourages us to move forward, to press on, to climb higher, and to go deeper into His grace and mercy. He wants our eyes to be looking ahead as He guides our feet by the light of His Word. He wants our faith to be trusting Him for new things as He does His work in us. He wants our obedience to be clothed with praise and thanksgiving as we follow Him into all our tomorrows. As His servants, He has called us to be faithful and to rest in His faithfulness. Daily, each of us has the glorious privilege of being able to continue on in all that He has called us to be.

—Roy Lessin

Continue On

... in your service

This is the day o

formed you . . .

made . . .

His Gift

This is the day God made.

It is His gift to you,

And through it

You can bless Him

In the things you say and do.

Reach out to touch another,

Let His heart be known,

Through your love

And thoughtfulness

Let His love be shown.

It is His gift to you . . .

*G*od was the one who formed you, gave you the breath of life, and brought you into the world. He did this so that His arms could embrace you, and His heart could love you. He wanted you to know that your relationship with Him would always be of more value than the things He would ask you to do for Him. He wanted you to be certain that He has loved you completely, before He ever asked you to do anything for Him. He desires that your service for Him never becomes a way of trying to earn His love or favor, but rather is an expression of the joy that springs from a thankful heart.

Because God orders your steps, you can always be assured there is enough time in each day to do His will. He sets the pace. He is never anxious. His purpose is for you to move in rest, live in peace, abound in joy, and be in total dependence on Him to accomplish through you all that He desires.

"Therefore, my dear brothers, stand firm. Let nothing move you. Always give yourselves fully to the work of the Lord, because you know that your labor in the Lord is not in vain" (1 Cor. 15:58).

Continue On

A woman once fretted over the usefulness of her life. She feared she was wasting her potential being a devoted wife and mother. She wondered if the time and energy she invested in her husband and children made a difference. At times she got discouraged because so much of what she did seemed to go unnoticed and unappreciated. "Is it worth it?" she often wondered. "Is there something better I could be doing with my time?"

It was during these moments of questioning that she heard the still small voice of her Heavenly Father speak to her heart.

"You are a wife and mother because that is what I have called you to be. Much of what you do is hidden from the public eye. But I notice. Most of what you give is done without remuneration. But I am your reward."

"Your husband cannot be the man I have called him to be without your support. Your influence upon him is greater than you think and more powerful than you will ever know. I bless him through your service and honor him through your love. Your children are precious to Me. Even more precious than they are to you. I have entrusted them to your care to raise for Me. What you invest in them is an offering to Me."

"You may never be in the public spotlight. But your obedience shines as a bright light before Me. Continue on. Remember you are My servant. Do all to please Me."

"Whatever you do, work at it with all your heart, as working for the Lord, not for men, since you know that you will receive an inheritance from the Lord as your reward" (Col. 3:23–24).

Through Me

*T*hrough me let there be kind words, a warm smile, a caring heart.

Through me let there be a willingness to listen and a readiness to understand.

Through me let there be dependability, steadfastness, trust, and loyalty.

Through me let there be compassion, forgiveness, mercy, and love.

Through me let there be every quality I find, O Lord, in Thee.

"Let us not become weary in doing good, for at the proper time we will reap a harvest if we do not give up. Therefore, as we have opportunity, let us do good to all people, especially to those who belong to the family of believers" (Gal. 6:9‑10).

The
Homemaker's
Prayer

Lord, teach me to say "Yes" to You in the daily tasks You place before me. May I take each one, whether it be cleaning, cooking, washing, or ironing, as a ministry unto You. As I do, may You fill each room in my home with Your peace and presence. Make my home a sanctuary and my heart an altar of worship as I serve You here.

As Unto Me

Others may not notice your efforts or give you recognition for something you've done. The credit may even go to someone else—do it anyway, as unto Me, for I am pleased by your service and will honor your obedience. ❖ There may be times when a job you have done will be rejected. Something you have prepared may be delayed or cancelled—do it anyway, as unto Me, for I see all things and will bless the work of your hands. ❖ You may do your very best, but your labors seem to fail. You may sacrifice time and money to help someone and receive no words of appreciation— do it anyway, as unto Me, for I am your reward and will repay you. ❖ There may be times when you go out of your way to include others and later see them ignore you. You may be loyal on your job and yet have someone promoted ahead of

you—do it anyway, as unto Me, for I will not fail you or make you ashamed. ❖ You may forgive others only to have them hurt you again. You may reach out to bless others only to have them take advantage of your kindness—do it anyway, as unto Me, for I know your heart and will comfort you. ❖ You may speak the truth but be considered wrong by others. You may do something with good intentions and yet be completely misunderstood—do it anyway, as unto Me, for I understand and will not disappoint you. ❖ There may be times when keeping your word means giving up something you would rather do. There may be times when a commitment will mean sacrificing a personal pleasure—do it anyway, as unto Me, for I am your friend and will bless you with My presence.

Continue On

... in your trust

Day *by* Day

Life's an adventure,

For we don't know how

God will direct us

From where we stand now.

We need only to trust Him

To show us the way,

And He will reveal it

In love day by day.

No Limits

There are no limits with God;

His resources are far beyond your abilities.

Never say, "I can't" without saying, "He can."

Never feel you are weak without knowing that He is strong.

You will never have to hold back or turn back due to fear,

Because He is with you—

You will never have to be defeated,

Because His victory is yours.

You will never have to settle for the ordinary,

Because His life in you is extraordinary.

He Takes Care

God takes care of the universe,

The stars and the heavenly host.

God takes care of the oceans

And the shores of every coast.

God takes care of the flowers,

Through the rain and the morning dew.

God takes care of everything,

And He'll take care of you.

Remember

The God you trusted in the past is the One who's faithful still.
Trust Him now, with all your heart, to be working out His will.
There's nothing that you're facing which takes Him by surprise—
All the things concerning you have not escaped His eyes.

His hand has been your covering through every circumstance.
Everything will work for good; nothing is by chance.
Let your faith abide in Him just like a mustard seed,
And you will find His promise true to meet your every need.

Wait on God to do His work in His perfect time and way.
The answer may seem slow just now, but He will not delay.
One day you'll see the wisdom that led you from the start
Was given by your Father's love to draw you to His heart.

"So do not fear, for I am with you; do not be dismayed, for I am your God. I will strengthen you and help you; I will uphold you with my righteous right hand" (Isa.41:10).

God's Path

W hen it's time to be obedient, take a step of faith—
There will always be a Rock beneath your feet to make

your footing sure.

When it's time to persevere, walk by faith—
There will always be a Light to show you

where to take your next step.

When it's time to overcome, take a leap of

faith—

The Father's arms will always be there to

catch you and place you safely on

His path again.

In His Time

I wait on God to bring to pass all that He has promised me,
And as I wait I rest in faith for all I cannot see.
For in His way He will provide at just the perfect time
Everything that's good and right to bless this life of mine.

**Look to the Lord
and you will always be facing
in the right direction.**

"For you created my inmost being; you knit me together in my mother's womb. I praise you because I am fearfully and wonderfully made; your works are wonderful, I know that full well. My frame was not hidden from you when I was made in the secret place. When I was woven together in the depths of the earth, your eyes saw my unformed body. All the days ordained for me were written in your book before one of them came to be" (Ps. 139: 13–16).

Before you were born, God was there, bringing you life and saying "Yes" to who you were and all that you could be. He put His arms around you even before you knew your mother's touch. He has cared for you as no one ever could. He has been your closest friend and constant companion—listening to your cry, enjoying your laughter, and encouraging you to follow Him. He has never shut you out or made you feel ashamed. He has comforted you and carried your burdens. He has given you grace undeserved and mercy that has been new every morning. He has been your God and friend, promising you a place with Him, in His house, forever. And as your Father, He has promised to be with you through all of your life with all of His love.

God Has Given You Another Day

God has given you another day

To hear the wonders He has spoken

To see the beauty of His face

To enjoy the pleasure of His company

To walk the pathways of His grace

To know the delight of His presence

To fulfill the desires of His heart

To discover the treasures of His love

What a day this will be!

I Heard My Father Say

I heard my Father say . . .
There is nothing too hard for Me.
With Me, all things are possible.
Do not be anxious about anything.
Trust Me; I will not fail you in any way.
You please Me by having faith.
I call you by name.
I will give you good gifts.
I hold you with My hand.

I heard my Father say . . .
I have placed My hand upon you.
Nothing that is good will be withheld from you.
You will dwell in My house forever.
I am for you—who can be against you?
You are My child.
I discipline you, not to harm you, but to free you from
every enemy of
Righteousness, peace, and joy.

I will not forget you.
Your times are in My hands.
I will teach you and instruct you.
I will guide you with My eye.

I heard my Father say . . .
Rest in My love.
I know you and I'm familiar with all your ways.
My thoughts toward you are precious, they
outnumber the grains of sand.
I am your provider.
I love you with an everlasting love.
I will bless you and make you a blessing.
I am your shield and protector.
NOTHING can separate you from my love.

"Cast all your anxiety on him because he cares for you" (1 Peter 5:7).

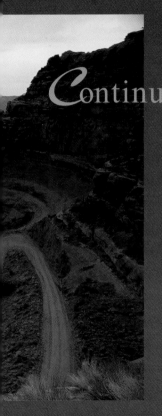

*C*ontinue On

... *in life's challenges*

The True Friend

A stranger may walk behind you,

But the Lord is your friend and walks beside you.

A stranger may be unfamiliar with your ways,

But the Lord is your friend and knows your heart.

A stranger may be indifferent to your needs,

But the Lord is your friend and cares about you.

A stranger may not know how you feel,

But the Lord is your friend and shares your joy and pain.

A stranger may keep things from you,

But the Lord is your friend and freely gives you His love.

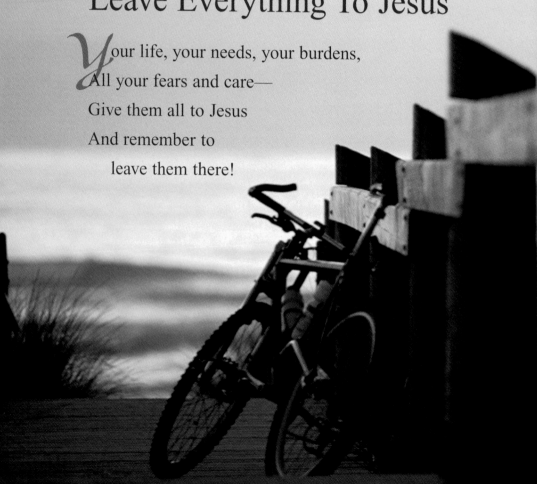

Leave Everything To Jesus

Your life, your needs, your burdens,
All your fears and care—
Give them all to Jesus
And remember to
    leave them there!

He Cares For You

*H*is mercy is able to heal each wound.

His presence is able to calm each fear.

His love is able to comfort each sorrow.

His grace is able to wipe each tear.

Touch Him

No wound is deeper than His mercy is able to heal.

No separation is wider than His presence is able to bridge.

No sorrow is heavier than His love is able to comfort.

No need is greater than His grace is able to supply.

Where Jesus Is

_W_here Jesus is,

We see light in the darkest place,

Hope in times of uncertainty,

Joy in difficult circumstances,

Peace in the midst of adversity,

Compassion in the presence of need.

Difficult experiences can lead us to ask, "Why did this happen?" But if we're trusting in Christ, we need never ask, "How could He let this happen?" God may not reveal all His reasons to us, but He has revealed His character to us. His character assures us that He never makes mistakes, is never uncaring, and never separates Himself from our need or allows us to be separated from His love.

Who Was It?

*W*ho was it, when your hopes were dashed and plans lay ruined, spoke in a still small voice of reassurance and put you on your feet again?

Who was it that brought you strength when the trials you faced seemed to rob you of all energy and hope?

Who was it whose protecting hand fought off all the enemy's onslaughts when you thought you would be devoured?

Who was it that surprised you with acts of kindness and concern when you felt like you didn't have a single friend?

In every answer, every deliverance, every provision, every surprise, every kindness—It was God!

Wings

I stood in awesome wonder as a butterfly took flight,

Spread its wings of beauty and turned away the night.

And as it passed before me, my eyes could clearly see

How God turns all my trials into special joys for me.

Jesus Is Triumphant

Jesus is better than anything
That others may call the best—
The peace that this world offers
Cannot compare to His rest.
Any work of the darkness
His power can quickly destroy—
What is known as happiness
Cannot compare to His joy.

All of the scholars' learning
Could never discern His mind—
All of charity's good deeds
Could never be as kind.
What many call the good life
Falls short of the way to live—
No possession is equal
To the blessings that He gives.

The applause that people offer
Is a very small reward—
No honor could be greater
Than the favor of the Lord.
All man's fame and glory
Fades in the light from above—
Where Jesus sits triumphant
Winning our hearts through love.

Jesus, You are better,
So much better than the best—
Your majesty and splendor
Outshine all the rest.
You are the King of Glory
The Lord above all kings—
Take my heart, my life, my all,
I give You everything.

See What God Will Do

What was the worst thing God had to face? The cross—the death of His Son. Yet, out of it God brought forth a river of mercy, hope, life, forgiveness—an unending stream of blessings for any thirsty person to drink from. What is the worst thing you face? Give it to God. See what He will bring out of it!

We should fear only if the Lord were not with us. The important thing is not to worry if your grip on the Lord is firm enough to take you through difficult times—remember, it is His hand that has taken a firm grip on yours.

"For I am the Lord, your God, who takes hold of your right hand and says to you, Do not fear; I will help you" (Isa. 41:13).

Continue On

... in your hope

*T*oday, God has you just where He wants you. He has taken care of every detail of your life. Your past. Your present. Your future. They all rest in His goodness. There is no chance, luck, or fate that governs you. Your life has meaning. Purpose. Direction. Hope. Today, you can rejoice. Know joy. Give praise—because His hand is upon you and you are kept by His love.

When the Good Shepherd speaks to His own,

He never uses words of despair, hopelessness,

frustration, defeat, discouragement, fear, confusion, or failure.

Instead, He gives His sheep words of hope, rest, victory,

assurance, peace, power, joy, triumph, and love.

Each day can be lived in beauty as you look upon His face.

Can be lived in hope as you lean upon His arms.

Can be lived in love as you rest beside His heart.

"He was chosen before the creation of the world, but was revealed in these last times for your sake. Through him you believe in God, who raised him from the dead and glorified him, and so your faith and hope are in God" (1 Peter 1:20–21).

The Holy Spirit,
Your Best Friend

I am the Holy Spirit, your Best Friend. I will reveal Jesus to

you. I am your Comforter; I give you power, I give you new

life. I am your Counselor; I am with you and live in you, I always

speak truth to you, I guide you in prayer. I am your peace; I fill

you, I pour God's love into your heart, I purify you, I anoint you, I

give you a taste of the good things to come. I am your joy; I assure

you of your salvation, I am gracious to you, I lead you in the ways

of worship, I make you fruitful, I give you gifts, I give you hope.

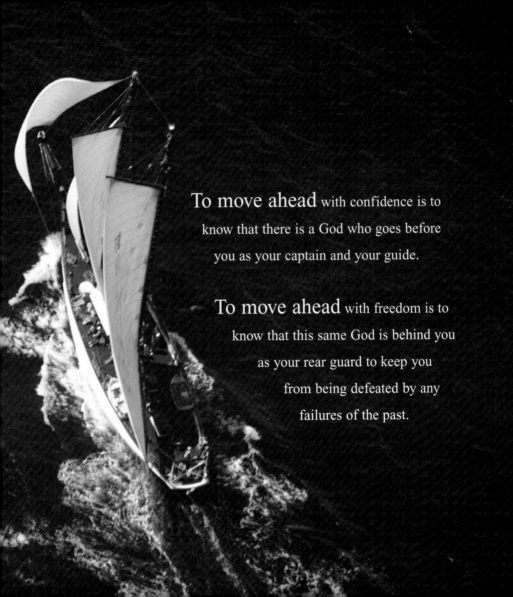

To move ahead with confidence is to know that there is a God who goes before you as your captain and your guide.

To move ahead with freedom is to know that this same God is behind you as your rear guard to keep you from being defeated by any failures of the past.

What It Takes

It takes a humble person
To call upon God's grace,
It takes a holy person
To look upon His face.

It takes a thirsty person
To drink the Spirit's wine,
It takes a broken person
To let His glory shine.

It takes a faithful person
To claim the heavenly prize,
It takes a seeking person
To make his thinking wise.

It takes a quiet person
To hear the Father's voice,
It takes a loving person
To make the highest choice.

It takes a willing person
To let God have His way,
It takes a trusting person
To walk with Him each day.

It takes a growing person
To listen and to learn,
It takes a patient person
To await the Lord's return.

You can touch Jesus with the hand of faith because He is near you, within your reach, even in the midst of the pressing crowds, or in the place of quiet isolation. His love is caring enough to respond to your slightest movement toward Him. Even when you've exhausted every resource and spent everything you had in search of an answer, He welcomes you coming to Him. He receives you as you are, even at your lowest point, or greatest weakness. His response is immediate, His compassion is total, His work is complete. His only desire is that you walk away at peace and free from your suffering. And because of this, the only place your thankful heart truly desires to be is at His feet in worship.

God Would Not

God would not have formed you if His arms could not embrace you.

He would not have chosen you if His heart could not love you.

He would not have adopted you if His hand could not bless you.

He would not have called you if His power could not enable you.

He would not have guided you if His resources could not provide for you.

He would not have led you if His presence could not keep you.

The Lord Is Your . . .

Shepherd, you are cared for.

Salvation, you are delivered.

Restorer, you are forgiven.

Defender, you are pardoned.

Teacher, you are instructed.

Captain, you are protected.

Guide, you are directed.

Provider, you are satisfied.

Deliverer, you are free.

Shelter, you are covered.

Confidence, you are assured.

Rest, you are comforted.

Delight, you are fulfilled.

Encourager, you are edified.

Victory, you are triumphant.

Rock, you are secure.

Father, you are loved.

He Has a Plan!

*T*here are many mysteries in life,
Many things we don't understand:
God doesn't always tell us
How He's working out His plan.
But in His time and in His way
He clearly lets us know
He's working out His best for us
Because He loves us so.

Just Think

Just think—You're not here by chance, but by God's choosing. His hand formed you and made you the person you are. He compares you to no one else—you are one of a kind. You lack nothing that His grace can't give you. He has allowed you to be here at this time in history to fulfill His special purpose for this generation.

"Let the righteous maintain a straight course and the holy continue on in holiness" (Rev. 22:11, TM).